"Ron's encyclopedic knowledge is built on a lifetime of experiences. His adventures become ours when he engages us as a master storyteller."

—**Kerry Sanders,** NBC News *Today Show* (retired)

"To millions of people in Miami and beyond, Ron Magill is the face and voice of all things wildlife. Ron's commitment to animals and their well-being is beyond reproach."

—**Mireya Mayor,** PhD, and
*National Geographic* explorer

# THE
# PRIDE
# OF A
# LION

# THE PRIDE
# OF A LION

## WHAT THE ANIMAL KINGDOM
## CAN TEACH US ABOUT
## SURVIVAL, FEAR AND FAMILY

## Ron Magill | Greg Cote

CORAL GABLES

For permission requests, please contact the publisher at:

Mango Publishing Group

2850 S Douglas Road, 2nd Floor

Coral Gables, FL 33134 USA

info@mango.bz

For special orders, quantity sales, course adoptions and corporate sales, please email the publisher at sales@mango.bz. For trade and wholesale sales, please contact Ingram Publisher Services at customer.service@ ingramcontent.com or +1.800.509.4887.

The Pride of a Lion: What the Animal Kingdom Can Teach Us about Survival, Fear, and Family

Library of Congress Cataloging-in-Publication number: 2022950417

ISBN: (hc) 978-1-68481-166-3 (pb) 978-1-68481-278-3

(e) 978-1-68481-167-0

BISAC category code: NAT042000, NATURE / Animals / Big Cats

**Ron Magill**

I dedicate this book to my wife, Rita, and my children, Sean and Alexis, for teaching me the true meaning of family and inspiring more pride in me than any person could possibly hope for.

**Greg Cote**

To my wife, Earleen, who has given me laughter,
loyalty, and love, two wonderful sons, and a life full
of gratitude.

# Table of Contents

# Introduction

# pride

/prīd/

noun

*a feeling of satisfaction derived from one's own achievements,
the achievements of those with whom one is closely associated.*

*a group of lions forming a social unit.*

**I look at lions as the definition of family. They really** are the only true social cat and, as such, share parallels with us that you wouldn't even expect from most mammals, let alone cats—traits that we generally think of as being anthropomorphic, but in reality, go far beyond what even some of our nearest primate cousins demonstrate.

If you look at the dynamics of a pride, you might think you're looking at a picture of a family barbeque. The females socializing amongst themselves, some of the aunts with the nephews and nieces, carefully watching over the cubs as they learn to play. Others might be out "preparing the food" as they hunt. All the while, the male, who might appear to be asleep on the "couch" is really on guard, ready to protect the family at a moment's notice. Whether it's the threat of drought, lack of food, illness, poachers, or any number of other challenges that they, like all animals, face, the aspect of protecting that family bond is front and center. Regardless of what might come their way, they face it as a family. As a pride. That fight for family and life is what drove me to this story.

Through my years, I've seen the different personalities in these prides that really drive home how similar we are. The unique individuals that stretch the spectrum of family. The patient ones, the macho egotistical ones, the shy ones, all working together to serve the family. I've been lucky enough to witness this firsthand, multiple times, and every time, I am blown away at the reflection of ourselves that exists in these animals. And I would love for you to keep that in mind as Greg Cote and I share this incredible story of K'wasi the lion.

When it comes to K'wasi, it is those very same personifications, but tenfold, that take this story from just being an appreciation of lions to a level that, if I had not lived through it and photographed it, I would not believe myself. In all my decades of working with animals, no animal has so profoundly touched me, in so many ways. From the deepest lows to incredible highs, it was such a roller coaster of emotion that, at the end of the day, it had to be shared. Everybody lives for that "happy ending," and in nature, that is rarely the case. So when you see something that gives you hope and inspiration to love deeper, you need to share it. And that's what K'wasi did for me. His entire life was such a question mark, and many times during his fight to live, we lost hope. But he never did. That valiance turned him into a symbol, for myself and for anyone else who has heard his story, of never giving up on life. Life is so precious, and when you have a family who is willing to help you fight for your life and save it, well, that makes it all the more meaningful and worthwhile.

Thank you for supporting Greg and me as we tell this story. I am not a writer, and Greg is a wonderful storyteller. He has a way with words that I hope helps you understand how improbable and inspirational K'wasi, and the animal kingdom, truly are. It's my mission that, by the end of this book, you see how we are all connected—not just in our ecosystems, but in our appreciation for life. People and animals have an unmeasurable connection that bonds us in many ways, and K'wasi is just the best example of that. There's an old saying that says, "In the end, we protect what we love, we love what we understand, and we understand what we're taught."

My hope is that this book can teach you that animals are so much like us, and thus, we'll want to protect them. At the end of the day, you might never see a lion in the wild, but that doesn't change the fact that we share this planet with them. And it is our responsibility to understand them and provide them with the quality of life they deserve. That's what makes this planet not just another floating rock.

**Ron Magill**

September 2023

**CHAPTER 1**

# K'wasi

Human love gets all the attention. It gets romanticized in poetry, glorified on Hallmark cards, spoken in languages infinite—but humans have no monopoly on the emotion. If anything, we have it easy. We have words. Animals feel every bit as deeply, as tenderly, as ferociously, but they show it with sounds. With their eyes. With mighty roars, and with gestures delicate enough to melt the human heart.

This is the story of a baby animal who struggled to be born, to live, and to survive, against all odds. Who endured adversity, tragedy, and loss. An infant who symbolized something much bigger than himself, and who relied on a village, on family and love, to save him.

This true-life tale invites the species of man and animal to venture closer to understanding, invites us to look at even the biggest beast, whether in the wild or in a local zoo, and see in those eyes not menace, but first a beating heart that is closer to ours than we have allowed ourselves to ever imagine.

This is the story of the extraordinary journey of a lion cub named K'wasi.

"It's what he represented, and not just to us. He represented hope for the future of lions," said Zoo Miami's Ron Magill. "Their populations have diminished drastically over the last decade. He was a symbol. The first male lion born at the zoo. It was historic. Oh my goodness. 'The king of the jungle.' 'The Lion King.' Everyone is raised with the idea of a lion with the crown on his head. Mufasa. That mystique.

"Well, K'wasi was *our* Lion King! It was going to be great. He was going to be such a highlight for the zoo. Everybody got so emotional. It was inspiring. Impactful. The volunteers, the guests, the press— everyone was so excited. I had worked at the zoo thirty years already, and finally we had a lion born at the zoo that we could watch being raised and share with the public!"

Zoo Miami, the fifth largest in the United States and the only sub-tropical zoo in the continental US, had been home to other major, notable births. Several gorillas. Komodo dragons hatching out. Their first koala. Baby rhinos. Even harpy eagles. But there is something about a lion. What the species represents to people. Its power. Its majesty. And this was a male!

"Our Simba!" said Magill.

But the joy at the zoo, near rapture over its first-ever male lion cub, soon was replaced by private dread behind the scenes.

"We all knew things could go south very quickly."

They did.

K'wasi was born on December 15, 2013, an early holiday gift.

But as the cub made it to one month old, not much bigger than a football, Magill was hunched at his office desk, fighting back tears.

He was drafting K'wasi's obituary.

A female lion cub had been born at the zoo just before K'wasi but had to be immediately shipped elsewhere. She had developed medical issues and her mother had rejected her, immediately and completely, so the cub was sent to Baltimore Zoo and was adopted right away. "We did not want to hand-raise her," said Magill. "That is always an absolute last resort."

Such is the unpredictability of animals, whether in the wild or at a zoo. Parenting is an inexact science, and one may or may not be suited for the task (as we humans might well acknowledge ourselves). Also, as with humans too often, a lion's path from birth to adulthood can be treacherous.

The zoo still was sad over the fast goodbye to its female cub when, as if a gift, a female lion at the zoo named Asha soon after gave birth to a male who would be named K'wasi.

But there were problems from the start.

The mother, Asha, had been pregnant once before, but with heart-wrenching results. She suffered dystocia, delivered one cub stillborn while the others died in utero during surgery.

Only four months later she was pregnant again, successfully this time, they thought.

Asha was a first-time mother, and the litter consisted only of K'wasi. Both facts sent up warning flags, as new mothers often struggle to adjust, and a lion litter usually consists of two to six cubs, not just one.

"First-time [lion] mothers are not nearly as successful raising cubs in the wild. There is a high mortality rate," Magill said. "But Asha dedicated herself. She was very attentive. We tried to make it not too overwhelming."

A new mother lion feeling too much stress can have dire consequences. So she and the newborn were separated by themselves behind the scenes at the zoo, away from the public. They stayed in a dark den. Only the zookeeper got quick looks in, but the idea was to leave them alone.

"What's very common is, if lions get stressed, they'll abandon and sometimes even kill their cubs— actually kill and eat them," Magill said. "This happens not infrequently in the wild. It happened at our zoo with our African painted dogs. The first litter she had, she killed them and ate them all. It is hard to explain. First-time mothers... There is post-partum depression in wild animals, too. So we wanted to be very, very delicate with Asha. We'd known she gave birth because we had a streaming camera in there. We could see the tiny cub in the straw and hay in the corner. But just one week after he was born, we noticed the cub was looking very weak."

K'wasi was pulled out and found to be very dehydrated— gently separating the cub from Asha itself a delicate maneuver that risked stressing the new mom.

"Pulling K'wasi away from Asha because he was dehydrated was difficult, a big challenge," Magill said.

"They worked really hard making Asha realize they weren't a threat, and keeping her at ease."

K'wasi had not been getting enough milk because Asha was not producing enough. With two to six cubs, there is ample stimulation to the mammary glands. With only one, "She kind of dried up, a common thing in some mammals."

They substituted Esbilac, a special feline milk. But how would they feed it to K'wasi? Would he accept it? And would Asha allow it?

The zoo would try anything to make it work.

"We didn't want to pull the cub from her and have to raise it—that was the last thing we wanted," Magill said. "No one can teach a lion how to be a lion better than another lion. That's the biggest mistake people make who hand-raise a cub. You hand-raise basically a psychologically unfit animal that doesn't know how to relate to its own species. That whole controversy came up with this *Tiger King* stuff. This guy is pulling cubs so he can take pictures and exploit the cubs for photos, and they had to be destroyed later in their life because they had no way to adjust to being tigers. That's why we only raise a cub as a last resort."

They managed to coax the infant K'wasi to a spot where they had inserted a bottle with milk into the link of a barrier. The cub started drinking. And Asha let him. Three times a day for several weeks this went on. It was succeeding.

"He could still be with Mother, and still try to nurse from Mom and have that bond. And she could still lick him and groom him and keep him clean. But we could make sure he was getting the vitamins and nutrients he needed."

All was well.

Until it wasn't.

During this time, K'wasi developed two extremely serious bacterial infections. "Quite frankly, we thought we were going to lose him."

Magill had done a press release when K'wasi was born, and the media were increasingly eager, "going crazy," clamoring to see him. The anticipation in South Florida was great.

But before K'wasi was ever unveiled to the public or press, "He really started to go downhill. I literally wrote a draft of a press release to announce his death. We had to be transparent in this whole effort. These stories don't always end well. So I wrote this release that K'wasi had died. I had it preapproved by the veterinary department."

There had been reinfections as well.

"He looked really bad. I've learned from experience that the animal can pass so quickly. I wanted to put my words and thoughts on paper when I could think clearly," Magill said of having the obit ready. "Because you become so emotional. I wanted a level head."

With Magill's crafted obituary in hand, behind the scenes, the supervisor of Zoo Miami's animal care management department advocated euthanizing the first male lion cub ever born at the zoo.

"I fought hard to not euthanize this cub," recalled animal care manager Ivy Brower. "I felt we could give this cub a good life."

Her boss reluctantly acquiesced, but fully expecting K'wasi to not make it.

"He thought I would learn a lesson from this," she said. "And I did. I learned a lot from it. But I don't think it was what he thought I would learn."

"I fought hard not to euthanize this cub. I felt we could give him a good life."

Brower learned that core spirit and will to live are something else animals can have in as much abundance as humans.

*K'wasi* is a common Akan boy's name in Ghana and is believed to be the name of a great historic warrior. True to his name, the fight in the cub began to show.

K'wasi, with great care and medicine, did get over his bacterial infections, and Asha did take him back (itself not a given).

But for the cub, Zoo Miami's Simba, the trials were not finished.

The heartache had not yet begun.

K'wasi was then three months old, healthy now and adorable, grown to about the size of a medium-sized beagle. The zoo exhibit with Asha and K'wasi had just been opened to the public, and it was a major draw.

"People were crying out of happiness," Magill said. "The place was packed."

Two weeks after the exhibit opened, Asha died on a table at the zoo's hospital.

"We noticed she had become really stiff. Seemed to be showing a lot of pain in the abdomen. Incredibly stiff and no longer paying any attention to K'wasi," Magill recalls. "She was not even trying to nurse him. They immobilized her and transported her to the zoo hospital, and on the table during exams she went into cardiac arrest and died immediately. They tried to resuscitate for over half an hour."

Sometimes Magill must stop himself and gather his emotions when he recalls certain things.

This was one of those times.

"It was so heartbreaking. When you heard K'wasi wailing in the back, *wailing*—it still gets my eyes watered. It still tears at my heartstrings. 'Oh my God, what can we do?'"

Suddenly, at three months and twelve days old, K'wasi was an orphan.

Asha had been born in early 2010 at the Bronx Zoo along with her sister Kashifa, who had given birth to four cubs a month after K'wasi was born.

The wheels started turning at Zoo Miami. In the wild, lions are the only true social cats. Magill and others thought, "Maybe we can get Kashifa to adopt K'wasi."

It was worth a try. Kashifa was producing lots of milk and doing a great job as a mother. It was a very slow process behind the scenes, but when Zoo Miami introduced K'wasi to the new brood led by Asha's sister—his aunt—it clicked.

*Family*, Magill thought to himself. It means something to animals, too.

For the longest time, and even now, science hesitates to endorse anthropomorphism, the attributing of human characteristics or behavior to animals.

Magill believes in it because he has spent a long career witnessing it, documenting it, *feeling* it.

He saw it again in how Kashifa adopted, cared for, protected, and raised K'wasi, the cub of the sister who died unexpectedly.

It offers a positive lesson for us humans when it comes to adoption.

"What is motherhood? It's not necessarily the blood that gave birth to you," Magill says. "It's who raises you, teaches you, protects you. K'wasi turned into such a wonderful lion because of his adoptive mother."

There seemed to be an instinctive bond from the moment they met.

"Kashifa seemed to show genuine interest with no aggression. And it's as if K'wasi was thinking, 'Who's this? It looks like my mother!' Not only did Kashifa accept him, but she seemed to almost favor him! It was as if she knew or sensed he needed special attention. He would never leave her side. Her own cubs, she pushed them away at times. But K'wasi would jump on her face and butt her head playfully. He could never get enough attention from her, and she always gave it to him."

Lions do not purr like domesticated house cats do. The largest cat in the wild that does is the cheetah. But if lions did purr, that might have been the sound of Kashifa and K'wasi with each other.

And the symbiosis was more than aunt/nephew.

K'wasi became a great big brother to his four adopted siblings. "He would rassle with them and pull their tails and jump on them, playfully knock them to the ground," said Magill, the eyewitness photographing it all. "He taught them how to be a lion. If he saw them fighting, he'd break it up. He was the consummate big brother."

The new, expanded family group was introduced to the public when K'wasi was four months old, all of them together playing. Zoo patrons swooned.

But the family was not yet complete. The portrait was missing something. The zoo had to do one more thing, and this presented the greatest danger of all.

They still had to introduce an adult male into the family.

Jabare and Kwame were brothers that Zoo Miami had gotten when they were one and a half or two years old, and Asha and Kashifa were later sent to Miami with mating in mind.

The loan and transfer, and occasional trade or sale, of animals from zoo to zoo is itself a little-known story. The vast network of American zoos adheres to what is called a species survival plan (SSP), which aims to bring together the best possible mates to produce the best possible offspring.

In this case, either Jabare or Kwame was the father of Kashifa's four cubs, but they could not be certain which one. Since they were brothers, a DNA test might have been useless.

"They loved each other growing up," Magill said of the male siblings, "but as soon as we introduced the females, Kashifa and Asha, there were epic battles. They became rivals who hated each other."

The zoo knew both males were breeding both females, but didn't know who fertilized whom. A decision had to be made: Who was the alpha male to get breeding privileges? Jabare was the dominant one and was chosen—a potentially deadly decision if the choice was wrong.

"I've seen it in the wild. Male lions will kill cubs they instinctively know are not theirs," Magill said. "They want to make sure their genes are passed along to the next generation. 'Survival of the fittest.'"

Lions are apex predators, known killers. If intent is there, they are merciless, and it happens fast. The signs are there to be read, and feared. The animal lowers to a crouch. The eyes widen with focus. The tip of the tail begins to twitch. When the ears flatten and are pinned back, that is the peak of pending aggression.

If you are close enough to see that in the wild, "You are about to be killed," as Magill puts it.

This was the risk as the zoo chanced introducing Jabare to his pride.

An additional danger: What if Jabare got along with Kashifa, but not her four cubs...or with her cubs (whom they believed to be his) but *not* with the adopted K'wasi? If so, K'wasi would have to be sent elsewhere to hopefully find another foster mother... if he survived that first-face-to-face with Jabare.

"We have to put whole prides out there. For cubs to grow up the way they need to, they need to have the whole dynamic, including the adult male also. Both sexes play a major role letting the cubs know what they have to be. Jabare was the dominant one, so we decided Jabare would be the one to be introduced."

Jabare seemed very curious about the four little cubs the zoo thought were his, but from a different den, not yet fully integrated. "The way he smelled them and chuffed at them told us they were getting along," Magill said.

But K'wasi was different. He stayed way back in the corner of the separate den, away from Jabare, who seemed to ignore him.

"We took that as a hopeful, good sign of his not being aggressive toward K'wasi," Magill recalls. "We did that for a week or so, and there was no displayed aggression."

Finally, it was time to let Jabare out of the den and into the open area with all of the cubs—with the pride.

"Once we introduced them, there was no turning back. If he was gonna kill a cub there was no stopping it, and it would happen in a split second. He would bite and kill them instantly. I've seen it happen in the wild. It's awful to watch. But we knew we had to do this for the health of the entire pride. We introduced Kashifa first, with her four kids and the adopted K'wasi. I remember it was an overcast day at the zoo. Then we let Jabare out..."

Now the adult male and female and the five cubs were all out of their dens and in the open together for the first time.

Jabare had not been with Kashifa for months. He ran right to her. They rubbed heads. He saw the cubs, and went to all four the zoo thought were his. He reached out with his paw, touched and smelled them.

"They were freaked out!" Magill recalls with a smile. "They screamed, seeing this massive head with this massive mane lean down to them."

The entire time, K'wasi hid behind Kashifa, never letting Jabare have a straight view of him. This went on the whole day. The other four cubs started to settle down, like, 'It's okay. He's Dad.'

"Jabare seemed to not even acknowledge K'wasi's existence. At one point Jabare crawled over a mound and kind of hid on the other side. K'wasi never left Kashifa's side. K'wasi looked around. When he thought Jabare was gone, K'wasi started to slowly walk away. All of a sudden you saw Jabare's eyes widen over the mound. He started running silently and low toward K'wasi. 'Okay, here it comes. He's going to kill him!' K'wasi screamed and ran and cowered behind Kashifa."

Magill, an accomplished wildlife photographer and national Nikon Ambassador, was chronicling it all as his heart raced.

All of a sudden, you saw Jabare's eyes widen over the mound. He started running silently and low toward K'wasi.

What happened next is emblazoned in his mind with vivid permanence, and imprinted on his soul like an indelible tattoo. He needn't recall it; it is with him, always.

The sound he heard made the blood in his veins seem to freeze.

"As Jabare charged, Kashifa turned around to him and roared louder than I had ever heard a lion roar, and with her claws out raked violently at Jabare's face. Jabare backed up, stunned, and started urinating all over himself. He ran away with his tail between his legs."

It was the power, in one incredible instant, of maternal instinct and the force of family—in this case not a mother's love but an aunt's—in full, feral majesty.

"It was like Kashifa was saying, 'Don't you even think about hurting him!' It was amazing to watch. My hair was standing up. There were tears welling in my eyes."

As Jabare skulked away, K'wasi by then had taken refuge hiding behind a tree, visibly trembling. Shivering.

"Kashifa sees him. And what happened next is the single favorite image I have ever taken or seen in my life..."

She went to K'wasi and took her massive paw—one that could kill a full-grown antelope with a single swipe—and gently put it behind the cub, pulled him to her, and tenderly put their heads together.

"I believe with all my heart," said Magill, "that she was conveying to K'wasi, 'Don't ever worry. I will always protect you.'"

Moments earlier, with no time to think, Kashifa's maternal instinct had been to put her life between her cub and an attacking male lion in all his power, one who might have torn her to shreds.

Now, that same instinct told her all that mattered was to lift her cub out of the trauma he had just experienced.

From that day on, Jabare never threatened K'wasi.

They spent the first two days at a distance, but on the third day, Kashifa slowly, carefully led K'wasi toward Jabare. K'wasi was still visibly afraid. Kashifa gestured, "Go to him now." K'wasi looked back at her with eyes that begged—"Mom, I don't think this is a good idea."

Jabare had been lying down, dozing, but now opened his eyes as the cub nervously approached.

For long seconds, there was still a fear that the alpha male might instantly pounce and kill.

Kashifa stood watching from afar, and if animals are capable of prayer, this might have been the time.

Moments passed slowly. Hearts beat fast. Kashifa waited.

She watched as Jabare opened his giant paws and tenderly pulled K'wasi toward him in an embrace. "To this day," Ron explains, "no one is 100 percent sure if Jabare is in fact K'wasi's biological father. Given the mating practices and the aggression that Jabare initially showed towards K'wasi (especially given how accepting he was of Kashifa's other cubs), the evidence indicates that Jabare instinctively felt that K'wasi was not his."

# CHAPTER 2

# The Hero and the Den of Curios

**Past the lagoon of flamingos, the animal lovers are** flocking through the turnstiles at the entrance to Zoo Miami in far southwest Miami-Dade County. To the right is an administration building, hidden by a high fence and a wall of trees. In it, down a long corridor, you hang a right and enter the room where Ron Magill's life and passion floods over you.

There is a desk in there, but "office" falls a bit short as descriptions go.

This is a den of curios and artifacts. A den of memories.

It takes a minute to notice that the walls are white, because they are covered nearly floor to ceiling and wall to wall with photographs, each of which tells a story, with framed honors bestowed and other signposts of a long, rich journey that is ongoing.

"These are all the people—I can't believe they've given me the time of day," he says.

On a high shelf are two Emmy Award statues. (There wasn't room for the other four he has won.)

On tables are wood carvings and horns and skulls.

Distinctive among the several dozen photographs is one of Ron with, unmistakably, "the King of Pop,"

Michael Jackson. In the background of the framed photo, on either side of Ron's head, are the majestic horns of a gemsbok oryx rising from the skull on the table behind Magill's desk.

There will be time for the story about Michael's private visit to the zoo with his children, but, first, Magill points to the photo nearest his heart. His hero is pictured there, casually holding a great horned owl.

It is his late mentor and dear friend, Jim Fowler.

Fowler was more than a sensei to Magill; he was an inspiration. He shaped Ron's career, and therefore his life, because, to Magill, the joy of life and the work he loves with such passion are inseparable.

Host Marlin Perkins was older, and mostly the show's narrator until his death. It was the younger, athletic Fowler who was hands-on with the animals and did the daring, thrilling stuff.

We are lucky in our lives if we have a guiding hand in what we all tend to think of as our fate.

"That guy was my hero. Catching caribou, catching jaguars, wrapping himself with snakes—I said to myself as a young kid, 'That's what I want to be.' "

Fowler would also take his show on the road around the country at times, contacting local zoos to provide animals. In 1985, the show was booked at Miami Beach Convention Center and reached out to Zoo Miami—then called Miami MetroZoo.

Magill was then twenty-five and had been at the zoo just a few years—he was there because of the spark Fowler had given him.

Now, someone would have to transport the animals to that same man.

"I was, 'Please, pick me!' I'd never been a person who was star-struck. But Jim Fowler was my hero."

A hawk and a crocodile were among the animals Magill brought to him.

"I was speechless. He was beyond a rock star to me. He was everything I wanted to be. Other than my dad, he was my idol. He became like an uncle to me. He taught me how to work with animals. How to present animals. And that if you learn to properly respect any animal, you should never be afraid of it. Jim presented animals in a way that planted a seed in me that grew into a tree of passion."

The meeting grew into a friendship that would last until Fowler died, at eighty-nine, in 2019.

Magill would phone his zoological hero in Jim's later years to stay in touch, and the voice on the other end would beam, "Well, shut the front door!" as a hello.

Magill visited Fowler a few years before his passing on his thousand-acre farm, Mud Creek Plantation in Albany, Georgia. Fowler lived until the end in the house he'd built himself in 1957.

Magill recalls Fowler's lament. The old mentor said, "The media is doing a very good job of trying to make animals dangerous. Today, the struggle for ratings is so powerful that the media feels the need to concentrate on gore, and that's unfortunate."

The cause is Magill's to fight now. He hates it when shows about animals use scare tactics with words like "deadliest," "attack," and "monsters"—frightening people away from nature, rather than helping connect them to it.

Magill remains in touch with Fowler's widow, Betsey. She says her husband adored Ron, and says, "He thought of him as a son."

On that most-cherished photo in Magill's office, the inscription in Fowler's hand reads, "Ron, the Earth's wildlife is fortunate to have you as its spokesman and custodian."

So many other photos, so many other examples of why, when Rod Stewart named his 1971 album *Every Picture Tells a Story*...he wasn't lying.

There is a photo of Don Johnson from his high-flying *Miami Vice* days, when Magill was an animal consultant for the iconic Miami-filmed TV show.

There is Sir David Attenborough, to whom Magill once presented the Audubon Medal at a banquet in New York. "The voice of nature," Magill calls him.

There are pictures of David Letterman, and Jay Leno. Magill appeared on *Letterman* several times. Leno called, but Magill could not go, so he sent a coworker who had the time of her life, but soon after was found to have terminal melanoma.

"I called Leno's production manager and said, 'Is there any way...?' "

The next day, the dying young woman got an encouraging phone call from Jay Leno.

When Rod Stewart named his 1971 album *Every Picture Tells a Story*....he wasn't lying.

Her husband said it was the last time she smiled before she passed away.

"That's why I think the world of that man," said Magill.

Nearby is a photo of Katie Couric. Another story. This memory is thirty years old, but it is not one Magill must work to recall; it is front and center in his heart.

Hurricane Andrew, a deadly category five storm, had left the nearby city of Homestead in ruins and ravaged the zoo.

"Katie Couric was the person who saved the zoo in many ways," Magill says. "After Hurricane Andrew, I did the live interview with her on *The Today Show* in the middle of the destroyed zoo and the whole country contacted us saying, 'Oh my God, we want to help!'"

Not with gravity, but with a smile, does Magill point out the photo of basketball superstar LeBron James and his then-Miami Heat teammate Udonis Haslem holding a twelve-foot albino python.

"U. D. [Haslem] loved snakes and LeBron tolerated them," says Magill. "The person beyond frightened of snakes, and especially birds, was Dwyane Wade. U.

D. would take the snake and run after him and Wade would scream like a little girl."

Another former Heat player who loved the zoo and is on the Den of Curios wall of fame is Shaquille O'Neal.

Magill recalls Shaq, towering in his crowded office, once phoning his guy at Pepsi, a major sponsor, and in that low, mumbly voice saying, "I need you to give some money to this man's endowment."

The Ron Magill Conservation Endowment soon received a $15,000 check from Pepsi.

We have not forgotten the photo with Michael Jackson, which Ron estimates was taken a few years before the singer's death in 2009.

A representative had called saying Jackson wished to visit the zoo with his three young children, Prince, Paris, and Bigi (then known as Blanket). There was concern about a crowd or paparazzi. Magill offered a private after-hours tour.

"I was preparing myself for a total freak show. I expected him to come with a cavalcade of bodyguards and people."

Instead, a lone black SUV pulls up. Inside are just a driver, an assistant, and the celebrity family. A heavily tinted window rolls down, and Magill hears Michael Jackson and his three kids singing, "We Are the World" in perfect harmony.

Michael wore a warmup suit with a Superman logo. He stood on tiptoe when posing for the photo. He was wearing what appeared to be a black wig. Magill noticed a piece of plastic under tape protruding from his surgically altered nose, saying he looked "like a wax figure in a museum."

But Magill also recalls that Jackson could not have been more gracious or thankful, and remembers how polite and well-mannered the children were.

As they parted, Magill told him, "Michael, you know if more people saw you as I did today, you wouldn't have some of the problems you have."

"The problem, Ron," Michael Jackson replied, quietly, "is no one will ever know what it's like to have to be me."

Magill felt sadness watching the black SUV pull away. The zookeeper is an emotional man, but in the world of animals that usually shows in positive ways, in uplifting moments, in good tears.

An example of that is his work on behalf of the harpy eagle in Panama, which he calls "the project I'm most proud of in my career."

Low on a wall in his office-den is a framed *New York Times* story headlined, "American leads fight to save tropical eagle." The American was Ron Magill.

In a celebratory ceremony at the newly opened Harpy Eagle Center in Panama, he was given a key to the city and named an honorary police officer. The harpy was announced as the national bird of Panama, "a grassroots thing I started," Magill says.

After the ceremonious event had ended, an indigenous man nervously approached Magill, carrying something hidden under a sack.

"I carved you this," said the man. "Thank you for caring for our bird."

Revealed was a gorgeously sculpted, stunningly detailed harpy eagle carved from the reddish-brown heartwood of a cocobolo tree. It is what Magill goes to and lifts carefully, as if cradling a newborn, when a visitor asks about his most-cherished memento in the room.

His first trip to Africa may be the best example of the power of animals to summon emotion.

He has been to the continent fifty-four times now. (How does he keep track? "Passport stamps," he says. "I have had three of them. They get filled up.")

His first trip was at about age thirty-one. He was with a guide in Maasai Mara in southwestern Kenya—a national game reserve larger in square miles than the cities of Houston and Los Angeles.

They spotted a zebra. Magill's heart began to race.

Ron was then a budding photographer who would go on to become an accomplished one. Today he is a Nikon Ambassador, one of only thirty-three in the US, and one of only two specializing solely in wildlife. (Google his name and "wildlife photographer" is the first description you'll see.)

Then, on his maiden sojourn to Africa, the sight of a single zebra in the wild caused a rush of excitement. His camera began whirring.

"Must have taken ten rolls, thirty-six pictures each," he recalls, chuckling at himself.

His wizened guide, with a small smile, advised, "You will see more."

Their Toyota Land Cruiser, specially designed for safari terrain, jostled and jounced over a hill and, suddenly, as far as the eye could see, tens of thousands of zebra and wildebeest were a rolling, ground-quaking carpet of thunder in mid-migration.

"I couldn't believe what I was seeing," Magill says. "I spontaneously started to cry."

Some thirty years later, the profundity of the moment still shows on Magill's face, in his eyes, in his voice, as he sits in his Den of Curios and reflects. He knows, and always will, that it all gets back to—no, *starts* with—one man. The one he saw as a young boy, through the looking glass of a twelve-inch black-and-white TV screen.

The grateful protégé's saying thanks every way he can includes funding a scholarship in Fowler's name at his hero's alma mater, Earlham College in Richmond, Indiana.

"My God, I'm living this dream because of him," he says. "Even after his passing, I hear him on my shoulder all the time. That man changed my life."

# CHAPTER 3

# The Lion King

**With a wink, he calls them his "movie-star checks."** The latest just arrived. The total: $19.46. These are Ron's residual rewards for having been an animal handler, consultant, or otherwise involved in several film productions over the years.

One was *The Lion King*. You may have heard of it. It did pretty well.

We'll get to that in a moment. Disney doesn't seek you out unless you first have built up a resume as a reliable conduit between animals and film.

The check for not quite twenty bucks reminded Ron of his work on a rather forgettable, small 1987 movie called *Five Corners*, filmed in New York. In one scene (spoiler alert!), John Turturro was determined to steal some penguins and give them to Jodie Foster to impress her. So they needed penguins.

"I don't really do that stuff anymore," Ron says now. "I've evolved to the point where we really should not be using these exotic animals in movies like that."

Then, he flew north with a bunch of squawking, braying penguins, and set them up in a contained area.

"I need those penguins to be swimming this way," the director, Tony Bill, instructed Ron.

"I'm not gonna do that," the zookeeper told him. "I wasn't going to put clothes on them or do anything to exploit the penguins or exacerbate their stress."

The director threatened to fire Magill from the set. Ron held firm. The director backed down.

Nobody knew it then, but there was a mole on the set from PETA, People for the Ethical Treatment of Animals.

"I got a letter from them congratulating me for not acquiescing to the demands of the director at the expense of the animals," he says. "For years after that, they would consult me about certain animal issues. I was very touched by that."

PETA has a negative connotation to many who see it as an enemy of zoos because the group is against any animals in captivity. And Ron believes "extremism at any level is dangerous." But that experience informed Ron that "there certainly are good people" in the group, and taught him a lesson he carries with him like an amulet: "Always do right by animals."

Very soon after that, Ron was invited to be involved with the movie *The Unholy*, a 1988 horror film. The scene: actor Ben Cross, in the grips of a nightmare, awakens to find writhing snakes covering his chest and belly.

"Ben was not very comfortable," recalls the man who traveled to bring twenty garter snakes to the set.

Ron had a plan to make sure the snakes would not "go crazy" during the scene and instantly flee from the actor's body.

"I had to cool them to shut them down."

He placed them in a sealed, see-through container in the refrigerator at his apartment.

There was only one imperfection with the plan.

"I didn't tell my wife I was doing this. She comes home to a refrigerator full of snakes."

Actually, Rita was then still Ron's girlfriend.

She screamed. Yelled, "This is where we put our *food!*"

"Honey, they're enclosed, they're fine!" Ron stammered. "I'm just cooling the snakes down. It's normal!"

Happy ending: "She married me anyway."

A new movie, not even titled or out yet, had just finished filming at the zoo. Ron had given the okay in exchange for the producer donating five thousand dollars to rhino conservation. (Ron didn't ask for it, but was cast in the movie for a bit part. He is seen as a news reporter on a TV screen.)

Until he got the call from *The Lion King*, the crown jewel of Ron's cinematic life was something he found right in his own backyard:

*Miami Vice.*

Ron served as animal handler for the iconic NBC TV show throughout its popular five-season run in 1984–89. It was his first experience seeing his behind-the-scenes work with animals play out before millions nationwide.

And this time, the checks were bigger than $19.46.

"Their budget seemed unlimited," he says now. "I would make more working an hour for *Miami Vice* than I would in a full week working for the zoo. I bought my first home with money I made on *Miami Vice*."

One episode involved "a bunch of tarantulas," but Ron's main job was handling Elvis, the pet alligator of

James "Sonny" Crockett, the show's detective played by Don Johnson.

"Don was never very comfortable around alligators," Ron confides. "It's why, as the series went on, less and less of Elvis was seen."

Five gators of different sizes were on hand for deployment, depending on the scene. All of the Elvises were on loan from Flamingo Gardens, a botanical garden and wildlife sanctuary north of Miami in Davie, Florida.

Once, the alligator-actor slipped unscripted off a boat into Biscayne Bay during filming. Gators are unaccustomed to salt water, which enabled its recapture. The salt made the gator buoyant enough to see near the surface of the water and recover.

Ron recalls Don Johnson being so nice to him that he got invited to the star's fortieth birthday party at the height of his fame.

No longer on a wall, but somewhere in Ron's house, is a photo from the party of Don with Ron's wife Rita.

"People would say, 'Oh my God, that's Don Johnson!' I'd say, "Yeah, that's who she left for me!"

Star power gravitated to the set. Ron recalls seeing Johnson and ex-wife Melanie Griffith rekindle their romance during a break in filming. Phil Collins, whose song "In the Air Tonight" became associated with the show, dropped by frequently. Barbra Streisand would visit while she and Johnson were dating. (Her assistant would advise the crew, "Don't approach her. Don't even look at her.")

Johnson had an introspective side.

Magill once overheard the actor, hearing the usual adulation on the set, tell someone, "Listen, this is just a page. I promise you tomorrow nobody will know who I am."

*Miami Vice*'s TV run was ebbing around the time Ron got an unexpected call from a man named Frank Gladstone, then in charge of animation for Disney's Florida operation.

*The Lion King* would later come out and shatter box-office records in 1994. This was years earlier.

"He didn't call it *The Lion King*. It wasn't close to being named yet. He said they were doing something that was basically *Hamlet* in animal form, using the animals of Africa."

The notion seemed far-fetched. High-minded, at least.

*The Tragedy of Hamlet, Prince of Denmark,* almost always abbreviated as *Hamlet* and written by William Shakespeare around 1600, was a tale depicting Prince Hamlet's attempts to take revenge against an uncle who had murdered Hamlet's father to seize the throne and marry Hamlet's mother.

To imagine this as the basis of a Disney animated film stretched credulity—at least then.

Gladstone told Magill, "We want our animators to be able to draw these animals the right way. To get their movements and everything exactly right."

Born in Miami, Gladstone knew of the zoo where Magill worked, and of his role with *Miami Vice.* He knew it was an open zoo, where his animators could see animals exhibiting their natural behaviors. All of the animals seen in *The Lion King* that Miami's zoo had in its collection, including the lions, would be drawn by the team of animators.

Ron was excited for his zoo to host the Disney crew. He had no idea several dozen animators would arrive in a caravan of luxury charter buses.

"I had no idea of the enormity of what this movie would become."

There were animators for every specialty. Some focused on giraffes; some did just trees, or clouds and sky. Some did lions.

"They would draw and draw, so fast, then take their hand and flip the pages right to left—and you'd see the animals move!" Ron recalls. "All of a sudden, they'd flip their sketch book like a deck of cards and you'd see a giraffe start walking. It was unbelievable. I remember thinking, 'Man, there's a lot of effort being put into this.' "

He was witnessing a lost art. Hand animation is rare in film today. Computer-generated animation has taken over.

Disney was so appreciative of Magill's role in what would become *The Lion King* that, in his crowded zoo office filled with mementos, you see a large poster for the movie, signed by every Disney animator. At his home is a limited-edition book on the movie and its filming, signed by the president of Disney and the artists Ron had seen making his zoo animals come to life in their sketch books.

*"I had no idea of the enormity of what this movie would become."*

He was a VIP guest at the movie's Orlando premiere in the summer of 1994.

Ask him the exact date, and this is what he knows: "It was the day of the O. J. Simpson chase in the white Ford Bronco."

It was June 17, 1994, and, as America watched O. J. and the Chase, Ron and Rita were watching the premiere on TV from their room at the Grand Floridian hotel, an upscale Disney resort. They were there with their toddler son, not yet two.

Not until that night could Ron appreciate the spectacle he was in for, or the scope and grandeur of what a major Disney premiere would look like. All of the Disney bigwigs were there. They had turned the company's Orlando studios into Pride Rock, from the movie. There were live lions there.

Rita had balked at going because their first child was so young. Ron inquired if the hotel had babysitting services and a Disney executive told him not to not worry, because it would be taken care of.

Before long, as they watched the O. J. chase unfold slowly in California an hour or so before heading down for the evening's gala premiere, there was a knock on their hotel door.

Within minutes, the entire room had been decorated with every Disney stuffed animal toy imaginable, including all of the latest from *The Lion King*.

Then the babysitter arrived.

Ron recalls the moment and gets a little choked up, almost thirty years later. He says, "When Disney does things, they do things pretty nice."

He opened the door.

In full regalia, in walked Mary Poppins.

# CHAPTER 4

# Twin Cats

**The story of K'wasi resonated with Ron Magill and** touched his heart in part because he felt he could see his own life story in the lion's. Crazy to some, perhaps—that a man might see his own path in that of an animal, let alone an apex-predator species. But there was a connection that Magill felt nourished his core belief in the strong commonality between animals and humans.

"Parallel lives," he says of himself and K'wasi.

Their paths were very different in a literal sense, obviously. Unlike K'wasi, Magill was not gravely ill early in life, did not then lose his mother to be raised by an aunt, and certainly did not have to fear an adoptive father might kill him because the child was not his own.

Magill had dealt with his own hardships, though, a past that was never known as his public persona and stature grew from local zookeeper to renowned wildlife conservationist making national TV appearances. (Just as the travails K'wasi endured might never have been known or shared had Magill not been moved to chronicle it all through a Nikon lens.)

In both the lion's story and his own, Magill saw a broader tale of perseverance. Of overcoming obstacles. Of needing help along the way—but ultimately surviving, and eventually thriving.

K'wasi, against the odds, would go on to live a long life that continues regally, with a family of his own and as the majestic centerpiece of a Southern Florida wildlife preserve called Lion Country Safari, located about eighty miles north of Zoo Miami.

"A spectacular lion today," Magill says, with what almost sounds like a father's pride.

Magill would go on to become a zookeeper, and later communications director, goodwill ambassador and the face of Zoo Miami, one of the biggest zoos in the United States. He became one of the world's foremost animal experts and advocates, a leader in wildlife conservation. He is this generation's evangelist for species that cannot speak with words, but that he believes speak to us in other ways.

It was not an easy climb.

Magill is from a family of immigrants, his father having left Cuba for freedom and settled into a small apartment in New York, where Ron was born in 1960. It was a family without the wealth to soften the transition. He was mocked and bullied as a child for his unusual height (he grew to be six foot six) and for his "foreign" background. He was taunted, called Frankenstein and "Magilla gorilla" and slurs less civil.

"The bullying thing was a really big issue as a kid," he says. "My first language was Spanish, and I went to a school that wasn't of a Hispanic population. It was tough. I was tall and lanky. Uncoordinated. Gawky. I was a scrawny little ugly duckling."

He sank into his love of animals as a refuge. A safe space.

At age five or six, Ron would sit cross-legged in front of a black-and-white TV set with a busted antenna in his parents' apartment and watch Mutual of Omaha's *Wild Kingdom*.

"That was my church," he says of the show that opened for him the windows of imagination and possibility.

Magill wanted to grow up to be Jim Fowler, that show's swashbuckling host. At an age when most kids were enamored with cartoons, watching the Road Runner outsmarting Wile E. Coyote, Magill's imagination roamed to Africa and thundering herds of wildebeest.

The love of animals was a portal through which he became an avid reader—"retreated into books," as he says. "But that kind of backfired on me, too. I skipped the fourth grade and it put me in with a group of older kids, making it that much harder for me to assimilate."

Throughout childhood, when he could not rely on going to school without being bullied or mocked that day, he could rely on animals and a reciprocal love that asked nothing in return.

His first pet was a dog named Skippy. He befriended a squirrel under a boysenberry tree in the backyard. And he lived vicariously through Jim Fowler.

The family moved in 1972, when Ron was twelve, to the Miami suburb of Perrine, close to where the zoo would soon be built and become the centerpiece of his life's work.

Just as K'wasi had to be introduced to a whole new family after the sudden death of his mother, "I was adjusting to a whole new world at twelve. I was no longer under the protection of everything I knew, and neither was K'wasi."

For the Magill family then, it was still a tough go financially.

"My mother using one credit card to pay off another," Magill recalls. His father was a contractor and carpenter who built the house they moved into, but they moved in before it was finished "because we couldn't afford to pay rent elsewhere."

His father planted avocado and mango trees in the backyard, intending to sell them for extra money but instead giving them away.

Magill grew up to be the first in his family ever to go to college. But his love of animals remained stronger than his desire for a diploma. He left the University of Florida in his senior year and never graduated.

In high school he had worked part-time at the Miami Serpentarium, first as a custodian, then a tour guide, and finally a curator of reptiles. Later he worked at Crandon Park Zoo as Miami Metro Zoo (later renamed Zoo Miami) was being built.

While at UF, "When I saw this new zoo was being built in Miami, I applied for a job. They called and said we have a position—but you have to come right now."

Magill's immigrant father had a third-grade formal education. To him, moving to America would be a passport to an easier life for his son. And so would a college diploma.

Guillermo Magill was a large, gruff man with a Cuban accent so thick it would have required subtitles were he speaking on TV. Ron broke the news of his decision to leave college to work at a zoo and saw his father's face wither to a look of anger and disappointment.

"You're leaving the University of Florida to shovel *shit*!?" he yelled.

Well, yes, was the answer.

"And I did. I shoveled a lot of shit. A *lot* of it," Magill says now, with a smile. "It was a way to get connected with these animals I love so much. If I had to be stuck in an office all day, I'd go out of my mind. So my first job was with a wheelbarrow, a rake, and a shovel."

His father passed away in 1991 from complications of bypass surgery.

*"You're leaving the University of Florida to shovel **shit**!?"*

Ron was then thirty and not yet what he would become, either in the zoo's hierarchy or beyond it, in terms of national stature in the wildlife conservation field.

"I'm very, very sorry that my dad didn't live to see me excel in my career to a point I know he would be very proud," says the son.

Years after his father passed away, Magill was given the University of Florida's Distinguished Alumnus Award. UF was founded in 1893, but fewer than 150 such awards have been given. Magill told the university president at the time, "You *do* know I never graduated, right?" The president clasped his shoulder and told him, "Son, your career is worth multiple degrees."

Magill calls that honor "an emotional pinnacle" because, for him, it was the beginning of closure to his father having been so disappointed that he was leaving UF early and forsaking a degree. Ron was later asked to give a commencement address to a UF graduating class at the O'Connell Center on campus.

His emotion that day?

"I hoped my father was looking down and saying, 'You did okay, kid.' "

In August 2023 (in the midst of working on this book), Magill and his sister were alternating shifts to be with their mother so she would never be alone as she lay dying in her home, after having been diagnosed with terminal cancer just the month before.

Lorraine Magill was ninety-two.

In one of Ron's final conversations with his mom, "She said she saw my dad and that he told her, 'It's okay.' She said it was time. She said, 'Don't grieve for me. I'm ready.' She was at peace."

She told Ron something else. She motioned him to lean in close. What he heard made him dissolve into tears, and his voice trembles in the retelling.

"My mom told me that she and my father have been so proud of me."

Saying goodbye to his last surviving parent made Magill reflect on the "circle of life" aspect that was so integral to *The Lion King*. It is yet another way humans and animals are alike: Life and death and, in between, the whims and unpredictability of fate, the reliance on others, on luck, on will.

"K'wasi lost his mother just like Simba lost his father," Magill says. "This cat was our little Lion King."

K'wasi lost his mother very early in life. Magill lost his late. K'wasi overcame an illness that nearly killed him. Magill overcame years of dispiriting taunts and bullying.

Zoo workers are always told to not become too attached to the animals. It is a mantra, literally a job requirement. It has no chance.

"It's not going to happen for someone working here with their heart and soul."

Magill wept over the years to lose animals by illness or naturally by age.

He wept for J. J., the silverback gorilla who passed away too soon from heart disease.

He wept to say goodbye to Toshi, who was the oldest black rhinoceros in the United States at the end.

Magill could not bear to watch as Toshi was euthanized. He had gone by the evening before, after hours. He knelt, put his head on that of the dying old rhino, and said goodbye. Today, in Magill's office on the zoo grounds, crowded with mementos, there is a special place for what at first glance seems just a nondescript heavy round of cement nearly the size of a dinner plate.

It is a cast of Toshi's foot.

With K'wasi, Magill had—*has*—that same very emotional attachment he calls "profoundly powerful."

His heart-deep passion for animals has told him again and again over the years that he made the right decision to leave the University of Florida to go "shovel shit" at a zoo, even as the pain of his father never living to see his success was deep.

That pain is why Magill tells this story, one etched in his memory.

He feels he has to. Because it is healing for him. The story means something.

A distant, early memory, this. The honking, bustling streets of New York City at night. Ron cannot remember exactly why, but he is riding in a car with his father. Searchlights were flashing across the sky. Ron thinks he was seven or eight.

"We drove by a hotel with big movie-star searchlights out front," Magill remembers. "There were limousines, and men stepping out wearing tuxedos. I said, 'Papi, what's *that*!?' He told me, 'That is the hotel where the very important and famous people go.'"

It was, in its heyday and height of glory, the Waldorf-Astoria.

The boy turned around in the car for a last look at the magical sight as his father drove away.

Some thirty years later, Magill got a phone call from Jim Fowler, his boyhood idol who had been host of Mutual of Omaha's *Wild Kingdom*, the show that first unlocked Magill's imagination and love for animals back around that time Ron had seen those searchlights in the New York night.

Fowler told Magill he was to receive a conservation award from the prestigious Explorers Club in New York. Fowler would present him with the honor.

The event would be at the Waldorf-Astoria. Hearing that hotel's name again gave Magill an odd chill.

"I felt like my life had come full-circle that night, walking into that hotel dressed in a tuxedo, walking to that stage in the grand ballroom. My dad had by then passed away. And here I was on the stage with my childhood hero giving me an award in the place where my dad had said, 'This is where the important and famous people go.' That represents for me what makes me the luckiest guy in the world."

Magill teared up accepting the award.

Later, Fowler said, "Ron, I knew this award meant a lot to you. But I didn't know it meant *that* much to you."

Magill said, "It wasn't just that, Jim."

Many years after that, on her death bed, Magill's mom told him how proud she and his father were of him. But it was that night, "where the very important and famous people go," that Magill had told his mentor Fowler, "I just felt my dad looking down and smiling."

The gangly child bullied and mocked, the one who quit college to "shovel shit"—he'd done alright for himself, his journey forever symbolized in his mind by one animal above all others.

Today, whenever he happens by the lion compound at his zoo, that animal is back in his heart. The tiny cub who nearly died, the one displaced but raised by the power of family and love.

"I always felt like the underdog," Magill says. "K'wasi was that underdog, too."

# CHAPTER 5

# Gratitude through the Endowment

The Ron Magill Conservation Endowment began in 2016 and has raised nearly three million dollars in the support of organizations and programs dedicated to ensuring that wildlife can flourish in the wild environments where it is naturally found. Through scholarships and more, the endowment also invests in individuals who share his own passion and are committed to becoming future wildlife conservationists.

Love of animals and a mindfulness of his own legacy were integral with Magill starting the project, but not what led him to do it.

Frustration and anger were that spark.

Seeing his own employer, Miami-Dade County government-run Zoo Miami, not doing enough was what led Magill to do more.

Magill always has had what might be called an anti-establishment streak, but might more accurately be called anti-bureaucracy.

He watched the zoo allocate millions of dollars for its own animal exhibits—such as fifty million dollars on an Amazon and Beyond exhibit—but next to nothing to promote and protect those same wildlife species in their natural habitats.

"It frankly pissed me off. And I don't care what the zoo thinks because I've said it to their face. There are many people, many at county hall, who want me gone. I don't toe the line. But if there's a real problem [with the zoo], I need to address that. The number one goal of zoos should be to ensure the animals we have on exhibit here can live in the wild. 'We're educating people' only goes so far. I heard that and all the other usual excuses. 'Well, you know, budget cuts, cost overruns...' "

It was government-speak he was getting. When Magill railed against the fifty-million-dollar Amazon exhibit allocating no funds for the actual Amazon, "I'd had enough. They said it won't happen again. Then we opened the Florida Mission Everglades exhibit for thirty-three million dollars, and zero went to Everglades restoration or any kind of conservation for Everglades animals. I lost it. It's in our own backyard and you have not allotted a single penny toward Everglades conservation or restoration!"

He was done with the status quo. Half in anger, half as a desperate threat, and with zero exploration of what it would entail, Magill told his bosses he would start his own endowment and do what the zoo was *not* doing.

"And you can't touch it!" he said. "These people are doing something wrong, and I was going to call them out. They said, okay fine, in a way that said, 'Ha, you think you're gonna be able to raise money? Good luck.' I left that meeting thinking, 'What the hell did I just do?'"

Suddenly the man who'd left college without a degree to go work at a zoo had cast himself as a fundraiser. He had assigned himself to build a charitable foundation from nothing.

The thought did not occur to him then, but he would come to know it well, and rely on it.

It would be the gift to him that in turn would become his perpetual gift to animals.

He was not alone.

He would have angels along the way.

One was Miguel (Mike) Fernandez, a Cuban exile, Miami billionaire, and philanthropist who in 2023 was recognized by the Carnegie Corporation as one of America's "Great Immigrants."

Desperation drove Magill to visit a man he calls his mentor—"a guiding light for me"—for advice, for suggestions.

"I told him I had raised $800,000 over a couple of years but had exhausted every connection I had. I told him, 'Mike, I'm at $800,000. You are well-connected. Do you know other people I can tell my story to?'"

Fernandez told him, "Look, Ron, you got a million dollars. What are you going to do next?"

Magill corrected him.

"No, Ron, you've got a million dollars," and committed $200,000 on the spot, saying that Ron would have the check within a week.

"Mike, I didn't come here to ask you for money," said Magill.

"Ron," said the instant benefactor, "that's why I'm giving it to you."

Having Fernandez's name alone attached to Magill's passion project gave it immediate credibility and heft.

"Mike, I didn't come here to ask you for money."

"Ron, that's why I'm giving it to you."

The Ron Magill Conservation Endowment, the one his Zoo Miami bosses had scoffed at as next to impossible, had taken off.

And its flight was just beginning, thanks to two more angels.

Their names are Mario Luis Kreutzberger Blumenfeld, much better known as Don Francisco, and Dan Le Batard.

Don Francisco is the Chilean television personality who for fifty-three years, until 2015, served as star and host of *Sabado Gigante* (Giant Saturday), the immensely popular, internationally viewed Spanish-language variety show. The show moved its base of operations to Miami in 1986, and Magill soon came on board as a longtime regular because the host wanted "an animal expert segment."

During his long run on *Sabado Gigante*, Magill also became a regular on the *Dan Le Batard Show with Stugotz*, for years a popular staple on ESPN Radio, before Le Batard left the network in 2021 and helped found Meadowlark Media, whose podcast network includes Dan's show as its immensely popular flagship.

The self-deprecating Magill is loath to admit it, but those two shows have given him a type of beyond-Miami celebrity and star power that in turn have led to late-night appearances with David Letterman, guest spots on *The Today Show*, and advisory roles on projects as diverse as the hit TV series *Miami Vice* and the epic Disney film *The Lion King*.

Magill in turn has risen to the list of prominent zookeepers and animal advocates, such as his mentor, Jim Fowler, along with Sir David Attenborough, Jacques Cousteau, Joan Embry, Jane Goodall, Jack Hanna, Steve Irwin, and Marlin Perkins.

And Magill discovered something he naively had not considered before launching his own endowment:

"When people recognize you, they feel they know you and are much more trusting to give you money. People see you on TV and it seems to give you instant credibility. Kind of sad, but..."

*Sabado Gigante* at its peak was broadcast in 156 countries. On a visit to Cuba, where his father was born, Magill was recognized and treated like a rock star because of that show. (It never hurts that he is abnormally tall, at six foot six, and has a distinctive mustache.)

Don Francisco today is eighty-two, living in his native Chile, and still on the air there.

"Ron was always so nice to people. I had chemistry with him since the beginning," Francisco recalled. "I found out from the audience that when we spoke in Spanish and he made a mistake, or when I made a mistake in English—people loved it, and we used it as a gimmick."

Beyond the good-natured fun, the host wanted the animal segment to be educational, and that was in Magill's wheelhouse.

"With Ron, it was not just the animals. It was the way you treat the animals and talk about the animals with such respect. For the young people, they are interested in how animals live, what they are doing, even how they get together as males with the females."

Magill believes deeply in the importance of educating children to know and appreciate animals. It is why he speaks to forty or fifty school classes in a typical year.

The animal kingdom may not have a greater living evangelist. Magill exudes passion. You hear it in his voice, see it in his gestures.

"My primary responsibility is to teach people to learn about animals so they can love and protect them," he says. "Our youth are sponges. You can make impressions that last a lifetime. It's a privilege to go to schools, to engage them and inspire them. I remember wildlife officers coming to my school in New York City, and the impression they made on me. Going to schools and hopefully doing that absolutely inspires me. Rejuvenates me. Their eyes are wide open with wonder, like, *Wow!* It reminds me of me."

For Magill it is all about paying it back, and paying it forward.

Jim Fowler inspired him. "Years later, I've had people come back to the zoo, and the greatest compliment and reward is when a kid comes back who turned into a wildlife biologist or something and tells me I inspired them to pursue their career. Now when I go to a school, I think, 'God, if I can do that for one kid!' "

On the *Sabado Gigante* set, Don Francisco would be delighted whenever Magill would, as a surprise, bring a variety of animals, from tigers to eagles.

The only animal strictly prohibited? Francisco was deathly afraid of snakes.

"I told him never to bring one! I'm superstitious about that. Superstition does not have a right answer."

Magill laughs, but warmly, at that memory.

"He was so afraid of snakes, one time there was a group of mariachi musicians, and he kicked them out because one had on snakeskin boots. You could not even *say* the word 'snakes' around him."

Magill's willingness to have fun while teaching about animals rose to a whole new level on the *Dan Le Batard Show with Stugotz*, where on his weekly segments he is liable to be asked which animal would be the last standing if an adult tiger, a grizzly bear, a rhino, and a jaguar were locked in the same room. Or what would happen if a whale accidentally swallowed you?

ESPN fought long and hard against Le Batard including an animal segment on his show, and lost. But it foreshadowed several disagreements with management that would see Le Batard eventually leave the network and set out on his own.

"Wonderfully cartoonish, absurdly passionate. He made the walls rattle when he walked into the audio-sphere," Le Batard describes Magill. "He was a symbol for us in many ways—that we could succeed doing entertaining things outside of sports. And that we weren't going to change as a show that was proudly and uniquely Miami."

Le Batard was aware of Magill through *Sabado Gigante,* but they had not met before he asked his producer to "get me an animal expert" and it turned out to be Magill. They became close friends.

"He's just so decent. Principled. Caring—beyond being a twelve-year-old who has grown up and is still doing a twelve-year-old's dream job," says Le Batard. "He carries himself with that kind of happiness. Someone who is good to people and animals, and good *for* people and animals. A pristine spirit."

Le Batard's show adopted the Ron Magill Conservation Endowment as its cause and mentions it every week, and the show's loyal audience in turn has been the main driver of donations, accounting, by Magill's estimate, for almost half of the near three million dollars and counting, overall.

The frustrations that led Magill to start the endowment in the first place continue. As recently as September 2023, he wrote an op-ed piece in the *Miami Herald* vehemently opposing local government plans to build a "Miami Wilds" water park on Zoo Miami land, because the land allotted was habitat for critically endangered species.

Magill was among the voters who'd approved the water park for the zoo back in 2006, "before we did studies on the property," he says. "We've learned a lot since then; 2006 was a long time ago."

Conservation organizations including the Tropical Audubon Society and Sierra Club have sued to stop the development.

Zoo employees, including Magill, were forbidden to speak out against it. Feeling he had a First Amendment right, Magill did not listen. When the battle is developers vs. conservation and environment, choosing sides is never difficult for Magill.

"If I end up losing my job, I lose my job with my head held high and my self-respect," he said. "I feel a moral obligation to speak up for what I've dedicated my life to. How can the zoo profess to have conservation as a main pillar, yet allow this project to continue on its own property? It is the definition of hypocrisy."

The threatened species affected are led by the Florida bonneted bat (the largest bat in North America) and

*"If I end up losing my job, I lose my job with my head held high and my self-respect."*

the Miami tiger beetle, along with butterfly, gopher tortoise, and snake species.

To the argument, "Ah, it's just a bat!" Magill notes that bats control insects that can carry disease and inflict massive crop damage. It's a circle of life thing. "We are all connected."

He likens species of animals, no matter how small, to rivets on an airplane.

"An extinct animal means a rivet is forever gone. Lose one rivet and the plane still flies. Lose enough and the wing falls off…"

Magill's outspokenness got him in hot water, again, with county and zoo management.

"I see a hostile work environment in the future," he said, ominously. "No matter. I refuse to say conservation is for sale."

He accepts the occasional turbulence amid the joy his career has been.

Magill pinches himself over what his life has become. Almost all of us can say we love animals or have had pets. But this man made a career of it that doesn't feel like work, because the work is where he finds his passion.

In vivid memories, he recalls how it started.

His first pet was a dog named Skippy, an Irish setter. There is an old photo of the dog pulling a sleigh during a winter in New York. "To have an animal that loves you no matter what, and never in a bad mood," Magill recalls. "Skippy was always happy to see me."

Those were days when Ron, at five or six, would sit cross-legged in front of a black-and-white TV set with a busted antenna in his parents' apartment and watch Mutual of Omaha's *Wild Kingdom*.

"That was my church," he says of that show, and the windows in his imagination the show threw open.

He remembers what he calls a "turning point." It was the moment his connection to animals felt visceral. Profound to him.

He befriended a squirrel. It was under a boysenberry tree in the backyard.

"In my yard one day I was able to take a piece of a peanut and con a squirrel out of a tree. It took the peanut right out of my hand and stood and ate it right in front of me. I felt a connection. Here's this wild squirrel, right next to a little kid. He didn't run away. He stood eating it, looking at me. Days afterward, I'd go out into the yard and he'd eat from my hand again."

It felt to him like he had a secret power.

"In hindsight, you're not supposed to be feeding wild animals. But to a kid who didn't know any better, I felt the squirrel was my friend. That he trusted me. He'd run away from other people. When my dad or mom came near, he'd run away. I felt like this animal knew me and I knew this animal. That little squirrel climbing out of a tree was a huge influence on me."

The early epiphany led to a life's devotion to animals, and to an endowment doing tangible good beyond the borders of Zoo Miami, a good that will continue beyond his lifetime. "If I drop dead tomorrow, that endowment is still going to be giving tens of thousands of dollars every year for the rest of time to protect the animals in the wild," he says.

In its short existence, the endowment has bought a research van for Audubon Florida's work in the Everglades, and a research vehicle for cheetah outreach in South Africa. Money has gone to buy radio collars for jaguars in Brazil. To fund scholarships for students doing conservation work in the field in tropical America and the Caribbean. It bought a research tower in the Florida Keys to track and help eliminate the pythons that are killing wildlife. And more.

Magill runs the endowment hands-on, with next to no overhead costs. He personally reads and vets the requests that come in.

Somebody suggested to Magill that chore sounds like a time-consuming nuisance. He shook his head.

"It's such a joy," he said.

CHAPTER 6

# Learning from the Animals

**Ron Magill has been to Africa on fifty-three** occasions. On more than one of those sojourns to the wild and wide open, he has happened upon a funeral service—but one unlike most of us have ever seen. He was struck by the solemnity, the stillness. There was a certain formality to it, and an unmistakable dignity.

These were elephants, paying respects.

Most recently, within Amboseli National Park in southern Kenya, Magill watched in silent awe from afar as a herd of elephants came by the remains of one of their own that had died months, or perhaps even years, earlier. One by one, in what seemed a procession, gently, with their trunks they touched the carcass of large bones. Some of those paying respects would make a guttural sound, almost a moan.

"I know those elephants were mourning," Magill says. "Showing reverence."

We hold such high regard for humans (many of us hardly deserving it) that we often demean our Earth's cohabitants as "only animals." As less than us because they are not us.

What Magill has been an eyewitness to in making a livelihood and a life of animals offers a perspective worth sharing. Because there is much we can learn from the animal kingdom.

Animals in the wild can be dangerous, deadly predators who hunt and kill for food, yes.

It is just as true that, just like us humans, animals can feel and care, hurt and love. And grieve.

Females run an elephant herd. It is a matriarchal society, with multiple generations staying together— what very few human families do.

The oldest elephants are most revered, and when the matriarch dies, it is one of the most somber events in the wild. She is the one who taught the others where the waterholes are, how to get to food, where to go when the rains come. The saying "It takes a village to raise a child" reflects the way of the elephant family.

There is a reverence for the past.

The scatter of massive bones found in the wild may have been there for months, years, or even generations, over time becoming its own cathedral.

"The elephants who come by, they seem to recognize those bones are from an animal they once knew, and continue to know," Magill says. "There is a wisdom in elephants. They don't forget that the remains are there. They come back and pay their respects. I've seen elephants come back with their youngsters who mimic the adults and gently touch those bones. It's as if the adults are conveying, 'This was a great member of our family. This once was an elephant that taught me what I know.' Elephants can communicate for miles through subsonic sound. They have a language we can hear, but also one that we cannot."

Witnessing these giants in such a tender tableau, it is easy for tears to well in human eyes, and to see in the elephants' eyes unmistakable love and respect.

Across the decades and continents, Magill has seen countless examples in the wild of behavior that showed the full heart inside animals, the capacity for love.

On one such journey to Africa, he saw a chimpanzee that had given birth to a stillborn baby, and for three days she carried the dead infant in her arms, rocking it, not accepting it was not alive.

"People who think that animals don't love or have these bonds and just do things by instinct—I wish they could see some of these things," he says. "Animals can feel that profoundly. 'Well, they're just animals!' No. It's not that way."

It was chronicling K'wasi's life journey that fully opened Magill's eyes and heart to the things animals can show us or, dare I say, teach us.

He watched that tiny furball of a lion cub nearly die from illness, recover, and then tragically lose his mother. He watched as K'wasi was taken in by his dead mother's sister—adopted by an aunt—and accepted into her pride. Then, most amazing of all, Magill watched as the dominant adult male lion also accepted K'wasi, a cub not his own, into that pride, something nearly unheard of in the wild.

"K'wasi's story is one of family and the culture of the pride," Magill says. "Lions are the only social big cat. All the others tend to be solitary. When a female lion gets hurt or too old, the rest of the pride will take care of her and share with her. They'll take care of the other cubs. On the flip side, if another male comes in and takes over, it's a horrific scene. That male will kill every cub that isn't his, to ensure his bloodline continues. That's why K'wasi being accepted by an adult male that was not his father was so unusual."

"People who think animals don't love or have these bonds and just do things by instinct—I wish they could see some of these things."

As with generations of elephants living together, the lesson lions can share with us humans is, to Magill, simple yet profound.

"It is that a family is much stronger than being alone. When you can depend on your family, you have a much greater chance in life. Life is difficult. The challenges out there are huge, whether in the wild or for us in everyday life. When you have a team behind you, like the pride, it gives you that confidence and security."

The K'wasi story also reminds that what constitutes "family" can be broadly interpreted to not just mean biological kin. Family can be chosen, too. Family is who surrounds you and provides support, comfort, and love.

Magill, through decades observing animals in their natural habitat and in zoos, has seen all kinds of behavior that reminds him of us humans.

He sees animals at play, rolling in mud, splashing in water, chasing each other around, using the enrichment toys provided in the zoo. Animals laugh, in their way. They make sounds that are joyful.

We can learn from animals to enjoy the moment, to act carefree.

"Animals are not worried about saving for their pension or what the weather will be like tomorrow," as Magill puts it. "Animals don't expect tomorrow. They live for today. I have learned that from watching them: Make the best of what you are doing every day."

The animal kingdom, despite its potential for danger, can also teach us how to avoid violence—a most valuable lesson for humankind, whose idea of problem-solving too often seems to begin with reaching for a gun.

"Animals can be really aggressive, but body language usually can solve everything before that," says Magill. "They do that with posturing, with silent communication. Animals read each other's signs. If a rhino lifts his tail up, he is not happy. 'Whoa. Back off.' Respect is something we can learn from animals."

With any cat, lion, tiger, or feline house pet, if ears flatten, the animal is on guard. If the tip of the tail is twitching, that signals imminent danger.

In the company of a gorilla or other primates, humans should never present a toothy smile or wide eyes and lifted eyebrows. These things are seen as threatening to primates, and to be aware and not do those things is to show respect.

Many birds—from birds of prey to storks, cranes, and swans—are monogamous for life, and raise their young together, yet another lesson for humans, whose divorce rate makes monogamy an iffy proposition. Birds have mastered the art of mating and relationships.

The bonobo, or pygmy chimpanzee, is the least violent of all primates and settles every dispute with sex. (If this isn't exactly a lesson humans can learn...perhaps it might be inspiration?) The sex of a partner does not matter to bonobos; sex is sex.

"The bonobos refute the notion that animals only have sex to reproduce. Bullshit! Animals have sex for pleasure, too."

Honeybees offer lessons in democracy, of all things. They depend on building a consensus with the group, with their decision-making involving spirited debate, whether the topic is relocating to a new hive or a change of queens. The hum of bees rising almost to the level of a roar indicates a colony in intense and perhaps heated discussion. But an agreed-upon consensus is respected, as in functioning democracies elsewhere.

Remember being fascinated by ant farms as a kid? You were watching tiny masters in the art of diligence and hard work. Resolve is in the ant's DNA, and lack of size only seems to underline that attribute. Ants rely on strategy and planning. They are skilled at organization. They store food when it is plentiful so they will not be without when it is scarce.

Mostly, perhaps, ants rely on teamwork. An old Frank Sinatra song called "High Hopes" references an ant who think he can move a rubber tree plant, with the line, "Oops, there goes another rubber tree plant." It alludes to an ant being able to lift more than ten times its body weight, so, in theory, enough ants *could* move a heavy object—thanks to teamwork.

The value of animals to humans is more literal, too, of course. There are more than 200,000 service and therapy dogs in America, some 50,000 police dogs, more than 5,000 dogs government-trained in bomb-sniffing and other skills, and about 1,600 dogs in the US military. Dogs are also at work detecting cancer in patients.

And the American Veterinary Medical Association estimates 63.8 percent of US households account for 48.3 million dogs and 31.9 million cats. Others considered companion animals include 3.5 million birds and 893,000 horses.

Most of us love animals. Not all of us treat them right.

The Indian political ethicist and philosopher Mahatma Gandhi once said, "A nation is best judged by how it treats its animals."

Magill would add that caring treatment of animals is very much in our own best interest.

"Whether it's bees, bats, and butterflies that pollinate plants that provide us with fruits and vegetables we eat, one-third of the food we put in our mouths is directly connected to a pollinator," Magill says. "Coral reefs provide protection for our shores and refuge as a rookery for fish. Amazonian rainforests provide us with oxygen we breathe and so many medicines we use. The bottom line is, we are all connected. By protecting these things, we are protecting ourselves. Just because we live in the city and don't see some of these things, it does not mean they don't have a direct connection to our quality of life."

Magill's passion is to spread this gospel, and that passion flows from him. He wears it as naturally as a lion does its mane. You hear it in his voice, which rises and quickens when he is excited. You see it in the way he gestures with his hands and arms.

The animal kingdom does not have a greater living evangelist.

"My primary responsibility is to teach people to learn about these animals so they can love and protect them," he says. "I think that *is* my job. The reason I started at [Zoo Miami] was not to work for an attraction, but to care about animals in the wild."

Magill says his "greatest compliment and reward" is when someone visits the zoo and seeks him out to say he "inspired them to become a wildlife biologist or some other career working with animals."

Magill laughs, shakes his head with a smile.

"I never thought of myself as someone who could inspire anybody. I was never the brightest bulb in the chandelier. Struggled to get Cs in chemistry in school. But I was certainly passionate about something. Jim Fowler inspired me. So I thought, 'God, if I can do that for one kid!' If I speak to a group of three hundred kids, that's three hundred opportunities I have to reach even one and make difference."

Even as Magill preaches that we should better understand animals, he is the first to emphasize how dangerous they can be. He calls that dichotomy "a challenge I've faced."

Earlier in his career, he'd always make guest appearances on TV shows holding a lion or tiger cub with a baby bottle. There was maximum cute factor, the show's hosts or audience guaranteed to swoon with *"Awww!"* on sight.

Only later did that begin to give him a bad feeling that he'd been conveying the wrong message. So he stopped.

"You show a cute cub with a bottle, and everybody thinks, 'I want one of those!' That's why for the last several years I have not done that. Baby cubs with a bottle are not like pets. People need to understand an animal is beautiful in its own right, for what it stands for and as a link in the chain that makes our environment healthy—not because they're cute. You can take the animal out of the wild, but you cannot take the wild out of the animal. Exotic animals do not make good pets. We should not be owning pythons, tigers, and monkeys—especially when companion animals [like dogs and cats] are dying in shelters because they're not adopted."

In that wrong-message category, Magill condemns *Tiger King*, that popular Netflix docuseries that so many Americans watched with time to kill during the pandemic. It explored the bizarre underworld of big cat breeding, specifically tigers bred in captivity and held in old-timey zoo conditions—in cages, behind bars.

Magill calls it "the greatest train wreck to come on TV," for two reasons.

First, it offered a misleadingly negative image of zoos in America, showing what used to be and still is some unregulated roadside attraction not sanctioned by the Association of Zoos and Aquariums (AZA), a nonprofit founded in 1924 dedicated to high standards in the areas of conservation, education and science. The conditions shown in *Tiger King* were a far cry from the wide-open, cageless holding

"You can take the animal out of the wild, but you cannot take the wild out of the animal. Exotic animals do not make good pets."

areas the vast majority of American zoos, including Zoo Miami, now have to better exhibit animals in their natural habitats.

Second, *Tiger King* seemed to normalize the dangerous notion of breeding, raising, and owning tigers as exotic pets.

Magill also condemns a recent animal controversy in his own South Florida area, at the non-AZA-accredited Miami Seaquarium, where Lolita the killer whale died after decades of captivity in a holding tank Magill said was too small.

Magill also criticizes a trend in media of exploiting the fascination animals hold for viewers.

Magill prefers to convey the dangers animals pose, not through scare tactics, but through education and understanding. And he holds strong in his belief that humans can learn much from animals because we have so much in common with them.

The belief is reinforced as he recalls the maternal instinct of K'wasi's adoptive mother to protect and raise him.

And as his mind revisits Amboseli National Park that day in Kenya, and the extraordinary sight of a herd of elephants coming by the massive bones of a deceased loved one to quietly remember, and pay respects.

"Feeling love and grief and everything else we associate with emotion—those things don't belong only to us," says Magill. "Animals feel them, too."

# CHAPTER 7

# Beyond Any Expectation

The way to Lion Country Safari from Zoo Miami is a straight shot north along Florida's eastern coast with a late jog west to Loxahatchee. Roughly ninety-five miles separate the two animal parks.

It took Ron Magill ten years to get there. It took lots of luck, but even more perseverance. It took family, and love, to get to where we were going, and to what we would see.

On either side of the long, narrow road into the safari park, there are large vertical posters of animals.

"There's K'wasi!" says Magill, as we pass the big cat's searing stare.

He has made the trek once or twice before to see the African lion who beat all the odds, the one whose life he has chronicled. It has been years, though. K'wasi is ten now. That would be very old for a lion raised in the perils of his heritage in the wild, if he lived even that long.

"The wild is brutal," Magill says, matter-of-factly.

With human care, some lions live to be eighteen or even twenty, making K'wasi closer to middle-aged now.

He wasn't supposed to make it to one.

He wasn't supposed to be here.

Magill knows better, intellectually, but his heart spoke for him on the drive north when he said, "I guess I want to believe he remembers me."

We are met there, and in a zookeeper's vehicle we drive slowly and wait outside the wide, electronically opened gate of the lions' compound, tires crunching gravel in the early morning. A voice on a walkie-talkie crackles, "Lion compound is secure. Stand by..."

The gate slides slowly open. We enter.

Lion Country Safari is an accredited safari park that allows cars to drive slowly among free-roaming animals including rhinos, zebra, and antelopes. The lions, though, may be viewed only from the safe side of a reinforced eight-foot chain link fence.

DANGER! the signs warn as one nears the Gorongosa Reserve—the lions' compound. PELIGRO!

The only other animals kept separate from the cars are chimpanzees, which can be rambunctiously aggressive and, in a mood, might think it fun to hop up and down on your Camry's roof or tear the windshield wipers off. So these primates are kept on an island, because chimps cannot swim and so cannot cross the wide, surrounding moat.

Lions are kept separate for very different reasons.

These are apex predators, maximum carnivores, the kings of the jungle. They lack stamina, but can run nearly forty-five miles per hour in deadly bursts if prey is in sight. And being raised under human care does not change their nature or instinct—does not take the wild out of wildlife.

An adult male lion can grow to ten feet long, not counting the tail, and weigh up to five hundred pounds. The bite force of their enormous canine teeth and the claws on giant paws, dwarfing the size of a human fist, are capable of ripping man or beast to shreds.

You know how our housecats have tongues that can tickle? "Sandpaper" tongues?

The papillae arising from a lion's tongue are longer and sharp, enabling it to tear meat from bone. The smaller female lions tend to be the breadwinners in the African savannah, the lionesses often hunting in packs. But the regal male is more than capable when its target is the likes of antelope, zebra, or wildebeest.

In the wild, the lion is known to sometimes cripple its prey and begin feasting first on the delicacy of internal organs before the prey is even dead.

We are watching intently, quiet in the car, waiting. The facility desensitizes the animals to its own vehicles, so it is as if we are not even there as the lion goes about the routine of his day, his life.

At last two lions mosey slowly into view.

The second is K'wasi. His coat is tan, his magnificent mane a bloom of darker shades.

Just ahead of him is a lion less familiar.

"Atlas? That's his son!?" exclaims Magill. "Holy geez! I cannot believe it! He's so much better-looking than his dad I can't tell you! A magnificent father-son!"

Atlas is four years old and already massive, bigger than his father. Distinctively, his mane extends across his underbelly. Atlas would not exist had K'wasi not survived. He is a gift. Magill last saw him as a small cub.

The two walk slowly to where our vehicle has parked, because it is near where food has been put out. This morning's breakfast includes large, hard-shell ostrich eggs and beef bones wrapped in palm fronds.

A lion's typical basic diet in human care begins with large chunks of beef, cow, or horse, but with bones, hair, and organs ground into it to more closely mirror what the animal would eat in the wild. Or a section of antelope carcass may be given to the lion. In the wild, when a lion has hunted and killed his prey—his and his family's food—the internal organs often are the first thing devoured.

"It's the circle of life," says Magill, meaning real life, not the Disney song.

Lion diet is carefully monitored and limited to about seven to eight pounds daily to maintain weight and health. There usually is one fast-day per week when the lion may be limited to a fist-sized knuckle bone to chew, promoting dental health. Frozen snack treats include "bloodsicles," which, mercifully, will not be further described here.

K'wasi especially enjoys what they call zip-line enrichments, food or treats presented above ground so extra effort is needed to win the prey. Bones are served wrapped tightly within fronds to make a game.

*K'wasi lounging at Lion Country Safari.*

*Jabare and his brother, Kwame, had epic battles to determine which would be the one to have the privilege of breeding with the females.*

*The battles between the brothers were extremely intense and totally contradicted the friendly relationship they had growing up together.*

*Once Jabare established dominance, he would shadow both females, Asha and her sister Kashifa, in hopes of breeding with them both.*

*At just three weeks old and with eyes barely open, K'wasi sat in a tub to get weighed during his neonatal examination.*

*K'wasi was gently held by the scruff of his neck as a stethoscope was used to listen to his heartbeat during his neonatal examination.*

*K'wasi at six weeks old relaxing in his secluded den.*

*K'wasi received supplemental milk through a barrier due to Asha's inability to produce enough milk on her own.*

*K'wasi explored his outdoor habitat for the first time when he was initially presented to the public with Asha.*

*K'wasi relaxing in front of Asha during their first day out in public view together.*

*K'wasi was curious about the public and his new surroundings but never strayed far from Asha.*

*Asha was very watchful of the surroundings and protective of K'wasi.*

K'wasi was always demanding Kashifa's attention once she accepted him as her own, often pushing aside her biological cubs to get that attention.

As time went on, K'wasi would venture away from Kashifa to play with his adopted siblings.

*K'wasi would often roughhouse with his siblings, which helped prepare them for the lions they were destined to become.*

*Being several weeks older, K'wasi was significantly larger than his adopted siblings and remained the center of attention.*

*Jabare was the dominant brother and was therefore selected to be the adult male introduced to Kashifa and all the cubs, though it was not certain if he was the father of each of them.*

*After greeting Kashifa, Jabare went to each of her biological cubs and gently pawed and greeted them.*

*Jabare would also smell each cub as if to confirm they were his.*

*Though Kashifa's biological cubs were initially intimidated by Jabare's massive size, they soon accepted his presence and were relaxed around him.*

*Jabare suddenly emerged from behind a tree to attack K'wasi!*

*After Jabare ran at K'wasi in what appeared to be an attempt to harm or kill him, Kashifa immediately lunged at Jabare and swatted at him with a tremendous roar that sent Jabare running away in fear.*

*Following Jabare's retreat, Kashifa slowly walked to a trembling K'wasi and, with her massive paw, gently hugged him as if to say, "Don't worry, I will always protect you."*

*In time, all the cubs relax around Jabare and the pride becomes complete.*

*K'wasi at approximately three weeks of age.*

*K'wasi as an adult at Lion Country Safari.*

Ostrich eggs are a particular favorite of K'wasi's.

On our visit, we watch as K'wasi settles in the canopy shade at the foot of a tall banyan tree, gnawing on a large bone, an opened ostrich egg safely nearby.

"Oh, K'wasi," says Magill in a whisper. "Look at that lion!"

A dozen or so vultures are skulking close (but not *too* close), hoping for abandoned scraps.

Son Atlas begins slowly walking directly toward his father, but stops as K'wasi looks at him as if to say, "Love you, kid, but do *not* come near my food," the look accompanied by a very soft, guttural growl.

Atlas detours, and softly settles eight feet or so behind his father.

"Obvious respect," Magill murmurs inside the vehicle, his Nikon softly whirring through the closed window. We are the length of the vehicle from where K'wasi lies in shady repose, a bone under one paw.

The park has opened, and cars of visitors slow and stop to ogle and take photos through the fence—even the sight of the safari park's star attraction merely lounging in the shade is enough to make fingers point, enough to make a memory.

K'wasi and Atlas get along very well. But, in the wild, male lions are kicked out of the pride when two or three years old to be on their own. It is why K'wasi had to leave Zoo Miami to be raised at Lion Country Safari, with Magill thrilled a zoo so close was available.

When K'wasi gets up to move elsewhere, only then does Atlas step up and safely settle in with the goodies his father has left for him.

Magill is watching the father, majesty in every step, full mane abloom, walking away.

"God, I remember him as the little cub we never thought would live," he says, voice wavering with emotion. "I was writing this cat's obituary."

Our Lion Country Safari host and guide, Haley McCann, calls K'wasi "the story I always dreamed he could be." His photo will adorn the cover of the park's next "Jambo" visitor's guide. It will depict a closeup of K'wasi's huge head, one eye wide open and staring.

"It's so good to look back to how far he's come," she says. "Quite a life this one's led."

Lest you think K'wasi is perfect in every way, McCann smiles and admits, "His roar is not the strongest-sounding roar. His is short and hoarse sounding."

Sure enough, he later stands and emits something closer to a gruff bark, a low, chuffing, grunt of a roar, hardly the iconic extended bellow of that MGM lion. Still, K'wasi is king at Lion Country Safari.

"As much as I shouldn't have favorites, it's hard not to," says McCann. "K'wasi is at the top of the list. There's just something about him. His look, his energy, just everything, He's my go-to."

She recalls the first time there was eye contact with K'wasi. When he looked not at her vehicle, but directly at *her*.

"Intense feeling," she said.

This is one lion.

Just one.

Why then is this animal, this one, above all others, so significant in Magill's life?

Magill, after all, is approaching fifty years working with and for animals, from those early days in 1976 when the teenager was a custodian among reptiles at the old Miami Serpentarium.

It isn't just that K'wasi was the first male lion born at Zoo Miami (although it *is* that, too).

It is what the lion represents, symbolically. What has been represented across pop culture, from the roar of the MGM lion in movie theaters to the animated sensation *The Lion King*. Not for nothing does the word "lionize" mean to lavish attention or approval on someone.

There is something special, iconic, about this one species. No animal more symbolizes power, strength, and courage—the very attributes we long to see in ourselves.

But the lion, even the *lion*, is not safe.

Magill has worked for a lifetime with wildlife conservation at the forefront of all he does, and K'wasi surviving against odds to thrive, and to have his own son, who himself will soon be a father, is the majestic face of what he is fighting for.

"What a legacy," he says.

Lions presently are listed as "vulnerable" on the International Union for the Conservation of Nature's Red List of Threatened Species. In parts of Africa, the designation is "critically endangered" because the populations are plummeting in such an extreme way.

The IUCN says that the current rate of habitat loss and poaching means African lions could be completely extinct by 2050. Africa's lion population has decreased by 90 percent in the past century, to about 23,000 left in the wild. Trophy hunters don't care. Conservationists had better.

So K'wasi may be but one lion, but he is one whose recovery from grave illness as a cub is a small triumph against the decline of the species.

"Zoos can serve as an insurance policy against extinction," as Magill puts it, noting there is a lion species survival plan in place.

(As we leave the lion compound, we drive past a scimitar-horned oryx, an animal extinct in the wild, a species literally being regrown, given a second chance at existence, because of accredited zoos.)

K'wasi may be but one lion, but he is one whose recovery from grave illness is a small triumph against the decline of the species.

It's crazy, even to Ron himself, where his life led, from the five-year-old boy sitting cross-legged in front of his folks' small black-and-white TV watching Mutual of Omaha's *Wild Kingdom* and wanting to be Jim Fowler.

Bullied, made fun of, growing up.

Going on to win six Emmy awards for wildlife documentaries, to be featured on Don Francisco's *Sabado Gigante* and the *Dan Le Batard Show with Stugotz*, and to have his own wildlife series, Mundo Salvaje (Wild World) on HITN, the Spanish PBS. To be featured on *Good Morning America*, *The Today Show*, and others. To have been on *The Late Show*, seated next to David Letterman.

This is the man whose father blasted him for dropping out of University of Florida to go work at a zoo, "to shovel shit."

A man who looks back on his career with smiling good nature and says, "I have been pooped on by more animals than I can explain."

Ron and I have known each other around thirty years; I'm guessing since the early '90s. He was the local zoo's media guy back then, and I had an idea for a fun, silly column in the *Miami Herald*: What animals would be best suited to be offensive and defensive linemen for the Miami Dolphins?

I remember phoning Ron anxiously. Had never met him. Knew nothing about him. Expected him to digest my ridiculous premise for a quick second and then bark, "I don't have time for this nonsense!"

Instead, he played along. Eagerly. Because, instantly, he saw an opportunity to humanize these big animals, as it were. The gorilla had the maneuverability and tactile function to block as a left tackle might. The rhino had the bull-rush force to rush the passer.

In the coming years, Magill's weekly appearances with Le Batard and elsewhere would bring him renown, not only for his passion but for his good nature and light-heartedness—always aware his mission to teach and foment understanding of animals could be done with humor, too.

"You started it all, brother," he once told me.

If they ever made a movie about Magill's life, they'd surely need to rewrite how he met his wife, because the reality is too perfect. Nobody would believe it!

Magill, in his early twenties, was the animal expert for the filming of a TV commercial that involved a Nile crocodile. The ad was for "Crocodile Mile," a slip-'n'-slide-type backyard water slide. He was youthfully careless with the crocodile, the deep bites on his right hand to prove it.

His rehab therapist at the hospital was Rita. He was smitten.

She found out he worked at the Miami Zoo. She'd been there.

"I hated it," she said.

They fell in love.

Their daughter works for iHeartMedia in Los Angeles. Their son works in Miami for Only In Dade, the popular citizen-journalism-driven social media enterprise.

Magill sees "a reflection, a parallel," between his own life and K'wasi's, hardly far-fetched from a man whose foundation for promoting better understanding of animals always has been a core belief in how much we have in common with them.

He notes he was an only son who went on to have one son of his own, and that K'wasi was the same.

He notes he overcame being bullied, "laughed at," while K'wasi overcame an early medical crisis and then his mother dying suddenly.

Magill has lived a life "way beyond any expectation I ever had. It's undeserving, but maybe I have become Miami's Jim Fowler. 'Our wildlife guy.' It's still surreal to me. I look at my life and I think, 'I can't believe that was me.' "

Then he looks at K'wasi today, and thinks the same.

He watches his magnificent, aging lion, son Atlas behind him, and remembers the obituary press release he'd written for K'wasi with tears. And then what allowed him with such gratitude to rip it up.

That majestic miracle lay before him now, *alive*, gnawing on a bone in the shade of a banyan tree.

# Acknowledgments

## Ron Magill

There are so many individuals who played a role in bringing this book to fruition. First and foremost, I want to thank my family for the unending support they have given me through this incredible journey with wildlife. I want to thank the late Jim Fowler from Mutual of Omaha's *Wild Kingdom*, for taking me under his wing and helping me to understand that animals are much like us in so many ways while teaching me that, as long as you properly respect an animal, you should have little reason to be afraid of it. It was an incredible privilege to have my childhood hero become one of my most important mentors. Special thanks go to Mario Kreutzberger (a.k.a. "Don Francisco"), for teaching me not to take myself too seriously and to never miss the opportunity to connect to a different audience while providing me with one of the most powerful media platforms on his iconic show, *Sabado Gigante*, that enabled me to reach millions of people around the world. I also want to thank Dan Le Batard and the entire crew from the *Dan Le Batard Show with Stugotz*, for their incredible support of me and my conservation mission, while allowing me the privilege of being part of their dysfunctional family and connecting with their countless fans. Of course, my publisher, Mango Publishing, and the entire team there for believing in this story and representing Miami so beautifully. A big thank you to my editor, Hugo Villabona, for guiding me and bringing in Greg Cote to help us tell K'wasi's story. There is no way that this book comes to be without Greg Cote, who I have been a fan of for decades. As one of the country's most beloved columnists, his engaging style of conversational writing provides the reader with intimate access to this beautiful story. Sharing it with him was a privilege and a pleasure. A sincere thanks also goes to Haley McCann-Gonzalez and the staff at Lion Country Safari for providing me the privilege of visiting K'wasi and his pride as he became the majestic lion that he is today, and the father of his own cubs. Heartfelt thanks go out to the entire Animal Health Team at Zoo Miami, all of whom always allowed me to be part of the many procedures and difficult challenges that K'wasi endured during this emotional roller coaster of a story. A special acknowledgment goes to Animal Care Manager Ivy Brower, who served as K'wasi's "foster mother" during some of the most difficult times of his life and whose incredible commitment and dedication is a major reason why K'wasi survived. This story would not have been possible were it not for her willingness to allow me to share some of Kwasi's most intimate moments and trusting me to document them to tell his amazing story. Last, but certainly not least, my most heartfelt thanks goes to my late parents, who though they weren't able to read this book, defined what love of family is all about and made tremendous sacrifices to enable me to have the opportunities to truly live my dreams and be able to share the stories that I have been so privileged and fortunate to experience.

## Greg Cote

What led to my thoroughly unexpected life began before anyone outside of my family and friends ever knew me. With a high school journalism teacher who saw a glimmer of writing talent, nurtured it, and is the reason I was the first in my family to go to college. With my older brother, who saw an ad in the *Miami Herald* for a part-time clerk in the sports department and asked if I might be interested. With Jim Martz, who hired me at age seventeen. From there, my career was on me, but not without help. From all of my colleagues, bosses, and mentors, led by the legendary Edwin Pope, whose elegant writing style was forever my beacon. Years later a friend, Dan Le Batard, welcomed me into his orbit of radio, later podcasting, opening up to me a second and invigorating career talking into a microphone. Across fifty years in journalism, the too many I have to thank starts fundamentally, always, with the readers who have followed me for so long, and the listeners who have come on board. The foundation of my career and everything built on it starts with our loyal readers and listeners. How might my life have been different had that one high school journalism teacher not identified a talent in me and taken the time to encourage me?

I think of that to this day. More recently, thanks of course to Ron Magill for entrusting my words to tell the story of K'wasi the lion and of Ron's own epic life in the work of advocating for animals and wildlife conservation.

# About the Authors

**Ron Magill** has worked with wildlife for over forty years. He was the host of HITN's national wildlife documentary program *Mundo Salvaje con Ron Magill* for several seasons. As Zoo Miami's goodwill ambassador, he has made frequent television appearances on many programs, including National Geographic's *Explorer*, the Discovery Networks, *The Today Show, Good Morning America, The Late Show,* CBS's *This Morning, Dateline,* and CNN, as well as on Spanish networks Univision and Telemundo. In addition, he is a Nikon USA Ambassador and has written and produced many wildlife articles and award-winning photographs that have appeared in publications and galleries around the world. He has traveled extensively throughout Africa, Asia, and tropical America while developing and directing conservation projects and Emmy Award–winning documentaries focusing on the wildlife of those regions.

Other than Zoo Miami and the Zoo Miami Foundation, Ron has worked with several children's charities with a special dedication to the Make-a-Wish Foundation, where he helps to grant wishes for children facing life-threatening diseases. In addition, he is a regular speaker at schools and civic organizations in hopes of inspiring others to follow their dreams while showing them the importance of protecting our world's wildlife for future generations.

Ron's proudest professional accomplishment is the establishment of the Ron Magill Conservation Endowment at the Zoo Miami Foundation. This endowment is the largest of its kind at the zoo and provides tens of thousands of dollars annually to wildlife conservation by providing annual scholarships as well as supporting field conservation projects designed to protect wildlife in the wild areas where it is naturally found.

**Greg Cote** is a longtime *Miami Herald* sports columnist who has been honored multiple times by The Associated Press Sports Editors (APSE) as a Top 10 national columnist. Greg has covered Super Bowls, NBA Finals, World Series, Stanley Cup Finals and, most recently, the arrival of Lionel Messi to Inter Miami. A previous book, *Fins at 50*, was published in 2016. A podcast begun in 2020, *The Greg Cote Show*, is steadily ranked among the most popular on the Apple Podcasts national charts. He also is a regular on the top-ranked *Dan Le Batard Show with Stugotz*. Greg lives in South Florida with his wife, an attorney, and their dog Charlie and cat Oliver.